TIME for KiDS

Spot the Difference

ANIMAL PICTURE PUZZLES

TIME for KiDS

Senior Editor, TIME FOR KIDS: Brenda Iasevoli

Executive Editor: Beth Sutinis
Editor: Deirdre Langeland
Art Director: Georgia Morrissey
Designer: Dirk Kaufman
Production Manager: Hillary Leary
Prepress Manager: Alex Voznesenskiy

Published by Liberty Street, an imprint of Time Inc. Books
225 Liberty Street
New York, NY 10281

LIBERTY STREET and TIME FOR KIDS are trademarks of Time Inc.

ISBN: 978-1-68330-836-2

First Edition, 2018
1 QGS 18
10 9 8 7 6 5 4 3 2 1

Time Inc. Books products may be purchased for business or promotional use. For information on bulk purchases, please contact Christi Crowley in the Special Sales Department at (845) 895-9858.

To order Time Inc. Books Collector's Editions, please call (800) 327-6388, Monday through Friday, 7 a.m.–9 p.m., Central Time.

We welcome your comments and suggestions about Time Inc. Books.
Please write to us at:
Time Inc. Books
Attention: Book Editors
P.O. Box 62310
Tampa, FL 33662-2310

timeincbooks.com

HOW TO USE THIS BOOK

Each puzzle in this book is made up of two pictures. Look closely at the picture on the left. Then compare it to the picture on the right. Look for objects that have been added, things that have been taken away, and changes in color or shape. For each difference you spot, mark one of the circles in the Keeping Score bar at the bottom of the page. (Note: when changes are made to things that come in pairs, such as eyes, ears, or legs, that only counts as one difference!) When you've marked all of the circles, you've found all of the changes. For an extra challenge, you can time yourself. See if you can do the next puzzle faster—or compare your time to a friend's!

CONTENTS

baby animals

Animals are everywhere, but one of them is real.
Can you find how they have changed, from head to toe to heel?

YOUR TIME

If all these stuffed creatures were alive, they might be sleeping like babies. Human babies snooze for about 16 hours a day, and cats for about 15. By the time he's grown into an adult, this human will need only about 7 or 8 hours of sleep. The cat will still need 15.

baby animals

I'd like to say they'll grow to be big, but they won't at all.
Can you find every Chihuahua change—even if it's small?

YOUR TIME

Chihuahuas are the smallest breed of dog in the world today. Named for a region in Mexico, these tiny canines are descended from an ancient breed called the Techichi. Techichi were prized by the Toltecs, whose civilization flourished in Mexico more than a thousand years ago.

baby animals

Picture one, picture two—so many things to track.
Can you find each and every change before this duck says quack?

YOUR TIME

Ducks stay dry because their feathers are covered in oil that keeps water out.
For the first few weeks, ducklings don't produce the oil they need to stay waterproof.
This downy duckling gets oil from its mother when they snuggle together.

baby animals

Penguin parties can be chilly, even when you're feathered. So we thought we'd switch things up. Now, that's a whole lot better!

YOUR TIME

Emperor penguins, the largest of all penguin species, breed during the Antarctic winter. A mother lays a single egg, then leaves to search for food. The father keeps the egg warm by holding it on his feet and huddling close to other fathers.

baby animals

Baby chickens in a line, waiting for their lunch.
Fuzzy feathers, beaks, and shells—what's different in this bunch?

YOUR TIME

A mother hen sits on her eggs to keep them warm. She purrs to her chicks and they cheep back. After 21 days, the chicks break free of their shells.

baby animals

Knit a sweater, play a game, tie yarn in a bow.
If you're looking for the changes here, search both high and low.

YOUR TIME 2:23

Few things are cuter than a kitten at play. But kitty antics are about more than just having fun. Cats are predators, and play is a way to practice important hunting skills such as leaping, pouncing, and stalking.

baby animals

A parakeet family, sweet as can be.
To find out what's different, check out all three!

YOUR TIME

This colorful bird nibbling her baby affectionately is called a sun parakeet. Sun parakeets mate for life. They are popular pets. But the birds are endangered in the wild due to habitat loss and trapping for the pet trade.

baby animals

Black and yellow, paws and webs, fuzzy nose and beak.
But that's not all that's different here. Come on—take a peek!

YOUR TIME

Baby rabbits and ducks are both fuzzy and cute, but they start life very differently. When it first hatches, a duckling imprints on its mother, or forms an instant bond with her, and follows her everywhere until it is grown. Rabbit mothers leave their babies, called kits, alone in fur-lined nests and return only to nurse them.

baby animals

What's black and white and full of krill? This penguin mom and chick.
Coming over for dessert? I hope you like fish sticks.

YOUR TIME

Gentoo penguins are found on the southern tips of South America, Africa, and Australia and the northern tip of Antarctica. Mother gentoos lay two eggs. When they hatch, the chicks are covered in fluffy down. It keeps them warm in the cold Antarctic.

baby animals

Here's a baby and its mom, both with fuzzy dots.
But there are changes everywhere—how many can you spot?

YOUR TIME 🕐

Fallow deer are originally from Eurasia. People brought them to other places around the world. Wild herds now live throughout Europe and the United Kingdom, as well as in parts of the United States, New Zealand, and South Africa. Fallow deer are born with spots; unlike other species of deer, they keep their spots as adults.

baby animals

These monkey moms and babies make a cuddly bunch. Which things don't belong here? I'll bet you have a hunch!

YOUR TIME

Japanese macaques, also known as snow monkeys, are found throughout Japan. These two mothers will carry their babies until they are about a year old. First they'll carry the babies on their bellies. Then, after about a month, they'll carry the babies on their backs.

baby animals

Let me tell you, little bear, how it's going to go.
We'll change the picture all around. And they'll never know!

YOUR TIME

A brown bear mother usually gives birth to two babies in her winter den. In the spring, mother and babies emerge to explore the world. Mothers spend about two years teaching their cubs how to survive in the wild.

baby animals

Mary had a little lamb—it would not stay the same!
Changes, changes everywhere. How many can you name?

YOUR TIME

The first sheep kept as livestock were probably descended from a wild sheep called a mouflon more than 8,000 years ago. Today there are hundreds of breeds of sheep. Fluffy lambs are usually born at the end of winter and are often thought of as adorable signs of spring.

baby animals

Koalas' pouches protect precious cargo from thieves.
Can you find other hidden objects in among the leaves?

YOUR TIME

Koalas are marsupials. A koala baby, called a joey, is born blind and hairless and about the size of a jelly bean. It spends its first six months of life protected in its mother's pouch. Then it's big enough to hitch a ride on Mom's back.

baby animals

Some folks think we're ugly, some think we're adorbs,
and someone made some changes here for you to find, of course.

YOUR TIME

Warthog families live in the grasslands of sub-Saharan Africa. When they are fully grown, these babies will have four long tusks for self-defense. But warthogs prefer running to fighting and can sprint as fast as 30 miles per hour. Warthogs are well adapted to life on the savanna. They are able to survive for months without water in the dry season.

baby animals

Baby lemur surfer stands on a rail.
Find changes to his eyes, his head, and his tail.

YOUR TIME

Bet you can't do this! This baby ring-tailed lemur is showing off his balancing skills. They come in handy in the lemur's native habitat: the forests of Madagascar. Ring-tailed lemurs live in troops of up to 25 animals, but their numbers are dwindling in the wild. Because of habitat destruction and hunting, they are now an endangered species.

baby animals

YOUR TIME 🕐

People have been decorating eggs to celebrate holidays for thousands of years. Ancient Persians may have been the first to paint eggs, as a part of the New Year celebration. Centuries later, decorating eggs became a popular tradition for Easter.

baby animals

Little goat, little girl—they'll become fast friends.
Things may change along the way, but we'll find them in the end.

YOUR TIME

Baby goats are called kids. You might think it's odd that they're called the same thing as human children, but goats were kids first. The word *kid* has been used to refer to baby goats since the year 1200. Some time near the end of the 16th century, human kids began to be called that, too.

baby animals

YOUR TIME 🕐

Although they look a bit like wild boars, lowland tapirs are more closely related to horses. When they are babies, their fur is mottled to help them hide among the plants in their South American rain forest home. As they mature, their coats become solid brown and they develop short trunks, which they use to pull leaves and fruit toward their mouths.

baby animals

Mama's white and fuzzy. Baby's just the same.
Finding out what's different is how you play the game.

YOUR TIME

In the fall, a mother polar bear digs a small den in the snowpack, then waits for new snow to fall and cover the entrance. She will give birth to between one and three cubs during the winter—usually in December. The new family stays together in the den until spring.

baby animals

Baby's as big as a full-grown man. Mama's even taller. Can you tell what's different here? If so, give a holler!

YOUR TIME

Baby giraffes are almost 6 feet tall at birth and can weigh 150 pounds. They live in herds of 10 to 20 females and young. People once thought giraffes were silent. But in 2015, a group of researchers from the University of Vienna proved that giraffes hum to each other at night at a frequency that is too low for humans to hear.

baby animals

YOUR TIME

Baby geese, called goslings, are ready to go, go, go the moment they hatch. They follow their mother into the water when they are just a day old. But it will be about three months before they can fly.

baby animals

What's an ostrich day care like? Do the chicks have fun? Of course! They've hidden puzzles here, for you to spot each one.

YOUR TIME ⏱

Ostrich chicks in the wild do not lack for friends. They are raised in a crèche—a large group of babies that is cared for by a single pair of adult ostriches. This gives the babies safety in numbers when they hide from predators and gives their parents time to forage for food.

baby animals

Hanging out in a tree to get a better view.
Leaves and toes, funny face—can you tell what is new?

YOUR TIME

Newborn chimpanzees weigh about 4 pounds. Like human infants, they are helpless and need their mothers to survive. Young chimpanzees stay with their mothers until they are 7 years old.

baby animals

Up all night, these little owls are red around the eyes.
But look again and you might find that there's a big surprise.

YOUR TIME

Found throughout Europe and England, tawny owls come out at night to hunt small rodents and birds. They also eat lizards, frogs, and insects. These fluffy owlets will grow into brown-and-beige adults with pale saucers of feathers around their eyes. Once they are grown, each will leave the nest to make its way alone.

fierce animals

YOUR TIME

Brown bears can be found in North America, Europe, Asia, and the Middle East. They usually prefer to be alone. They do not defend any specific territories but will attack any other bears that come too close.

fierce animals

Come a little closer—I'll show you my jaws.
Lean in to look for changes. Please don't mind the claws.

YOUR TIME

Majestic mountain lions, also called cougars or pumas, can be found from northern Canada all the way to the very southern tip of Chile, in South America. They disappeared from the eastern United States after people hunted them, but they may be making a comeback there, too.

fierce animals

YOUR TIME 🕐

Gray wolves, also called timber wolves, once roamed throughout all of North America. They were hunted to near extinction. Today the top predators are making a comeback, mainly in the western United States. They also make their home in Canada, Europe, and Asia.

fierce animals

YOUR TIME

Amur tigers are the largest cats in the world. In the 1940s, there were only about 40 left in the wild. After decades of government protection, there are now about 500 Amur tigers living in the remote woods of Siberia, in Russia.

fierce animals

Look for changes all around this fearsome grizzly bear.
But if you're swimming in his stream, please proceed with care.

YOUR TIME

The largest brown bears in the world can be found in western Alaska and British Columbia, Canada, where there is plenty of meat and fish for them to eat. North American brown bears grow to be about 8 feet long and can weigh up to 800 pounds.

fierce animals

Can't spot the difference? You should have my eyes. I can spot a tiny mouse from high up in the sky.

YOUR TIME

With wings that can measure up to 4 feet across, the red-tailed hawk prowls the North American skies in search of prey. After spotting a small mammal, bird, or reptile from a high perch or in flight, it swoops down and snatches the animal up in its talons.

fierce animals

Come a little closer! Are you worried that I'll bite?
Lean as near as you would like—but warning! I just might!

YOUR TIME

A crocodile is an ambush predator. The position of its eyes on top of its head allow it to hide beneath the water, yet still see prey above it. When an unsuspecting animal comes near, the crocodile uses its tail to lunge forward and snatch the prey in its powerful jaws.

fierce animals

🔍 Arctic wolves are masters at hiding in the snow. They've hidden changes everywhere. Count them as you go!

YOUR TIME 🕐

Arctic wolves, often called polar wolves, live in the frigid Arctic regions of North America and Greenland. Since they live in cold, remote areas, Arctic wolves needn't fear humans. But their habitat is threatened by climate change.

fierce animals

Some say I'm the fiercest fish swimming in the sea.
But I can change—already have! Take a look at me!

YOUR TIME

Camouflaged by stripes, lionfish blend into the backgrounds of their homes in the Atlantic and Indian Oceans. When tasty fish or shrimp swim by, lionfish swallow them whole. Lionfish are also well armed against attack. Venomous spines hidden in their fins make them potentially deadly snacks for larger predators.

fierce animals

YOUR TIME

Great hammerhead sharks can grow to be as long as 18 feet and weigh up to 1,000 pounds. They are well designed for hunting. Their wide-placed eyes give them large fields of vision. Their broad snouts contain special organs that detect electric signals emitted from prey. Luckily for us, they rarely bite humans.

fierce animals

Who needs fangs when you're a fierce rat catcher in the trees? Find what else is missing. It should be a breeze.

YOUR TIME

The red-tailed racer, also known as the red-tailed green rat snake, lives in the trees of southeast Asia, where it eats birds, bats, and rats. It may not be venomous, but this 7-foot-long monster still looks terribly fierce.

fierce animals

I may look bright and cheerful, but I am full of tricks.
Want to know how fierce I am? Come close and take a lick.

YOUR TIME

The black-legged poison frog may look cute, but it is armed and dangerous. It secretes a deadly toxin through its skin. The frog needs its native food sources, such as ants and termites, to produce the poison. This species is endangered in the wild. It is found only in a tiny area of Colombia, South America.

fierce animals

Count the changes if you can—you'd better do it soon.
This kind of devil isn't feisty only in cartoons!

YOUR TIME

A Tasmanian devil is about the size of a large cat, weighing between 13 and 18 pounds. It may have gotten its ferocious name because it bares its teeth when threatened, or perhaps because it snarls and screams when feeding at night. This meat-eating marsupial is now found only on the island of Tasmania, Australia.

fierce animals

Black and white, flashing fins, leaping through the air.
Can you find everything that's different in this pair?

YOUR TIME

People tend to think of orcas, the largest dolphins, as friendly entertainers. But they are powerful and clever hunters, snapping up seals, walruses, penguins, fish, and pretty much anything that moves in the ocean. Orcas can measure 32 feet long and weigh 12,000 pounds. This is one dolphin you'll want to avoid!

fierce animals

YOUR TIME

A white rhinoceros isn't white at all. Its name comes from the word *weit*, which means "wide" in Africaans and refers to the shape of its upper lip. (The black rhinoceros has a pointed lip.) The white rhino is a conservation success story. It was nearly extinct in the 1800s, but now there are more than 20,000 in the wild.

fierce animals

I can make YOU different if you'll climb into my web.
I'll wrap you up in finest silk and weave a comfy bed.

YOUR TIME

The familiar spiral shape of this spiderweb is the mark of an orb weaver, a common type of spider. There are more than 3,000 species of orb weavers found throughout the world. Their sticky webs capture unsuspecting insects, which the spiders then paralyze with their venom. What happens next? Lunchtime.

fierce animals

This monkey looks as though a clown helped it with its makeup. Can you find what's different in this mandrill photo shake-up?

YOUR TIME

Mandrills are found in central West Africa. Their fierce facial colors and long, sharp fangs make them look pretty intimidating. Mandrills are forest dwellers and vegetarians, scavenging for plants and fruits 15 feet high up in the trees.

fierce animals

YOUR TIME 🕐

Jaguars are the largest cats in the Western Hemisphere. From the tips of their noses to the ends of their tails, they can measure up to 7 feet long. The stealthy hunters live along the border between the United States and Mexico, and all the way down to Argentina. They are strong swimmers and often catch fish and turtles to eat.

fierce animals

Dinosaurs were scary beasts, but there's no need to fear.
Like much in this dino scene, they're no longer here!

YOUR TIME 🕐

Some of the fiercest animals of all time lived 75 million years ago, during the Cretaceous period. The velociraptor probably weighed only 30 pounds—about as big as a medium-size dog. But it was likely an intelligent and capable hunter, and may have been covered in feathers.

fierce animals

Don't go near his water hole, if you know what's good for you. Count the changes and skedaddle. That's all you can do!

YOUR TIME

Portly hippopotamuses don't look like they are built for the water, but their name means "water horse" for a reason. Although a male hippo can weigh 10,000 pounds, and cannot swim, he moves quickly through the water by taking giant underwater leaps.

fierce animals

You can look for each and every photo change we made.
But if this fellow changes rings, you'd better be afraid!

YOUR TIME

There are 10 species of blue-ringed octopuses. The largest is only about 4 inches from the tip of one arm to the tip of another. It mostly prefers to use its mottled brown skin to hide among the rocks. But when this creature feels threatened, it flashes bright blue rings. Don't be fooled by its size. A bite from this tiny animal can kill a human.

fierce animals

There are changes everywhere. See what you can see.
But if you're hiking in the woods, please don't step on me!

YOUR TIME

Western rattlesnakes live throughout the American West, and are well equipped for hunting. They have excellent camouflage, body-heat sensors, and forward-facing eyes that allow them to strike more accurately than many other snakes. Still, they prefer not to have to bite humans. Stay out of their way, and they'll stay out of yours.

fierce animals

YOUR TIME

About 30 species of piranhas, such as these red-bellied piranhas, can be found in rivers throughout South America. Despite their fierce reputation, not all rely on meat. Some are omnivores and some eat only plants. All pack a ferocious bite, with sharp, interlocking teeth and jaws that can deliver about 72 pounds of force.

fierce animals

Look for everything that's different; count up what is new.
But while you're checking out the ground, don't let him step on you!

YOUR TIME

African elephants, weighing in at as much as 13,000 pounds, are the largest land animals on Earth. They are found throughout sub-Saharan Africa. They can be divided into two groups. Savanna elephants live in the grasslands. Forest elephants are smaller and live in wooded areas in the Congo basin.

fierce animals

YOUR TIME

There are more than 200 species of moray eels. Each has a wicked bite. This snakelike fish has two sets of jaws. The first set holds its prey in place. The second set comes out of the throat to drag the prey into its mouth.

friendly animals

Tropical butterflies, five different kinds.
There are ten changes here—how many can you find?

YOUR TIME

There are about 20,000 species of butterflies found throughout the world. They can be huge, like the Queen Alexandra's birdwing. Its wings measure up to 10 inches from tip to tip. They can also be teeny-tiny. The western pygmy blue measures just a half-inch across.

friendly animals

YOUR TIME

Dogs may have first started living with humans about 32,000 years ago. Cats, on the other hand, weren't domesticated until about 12,000 years ago. Even so, the two usually get along pretty well.

friendly animals

We'll ride into the sunset, my pony pal and I.
And on the way we'll see how many changes we can spy.

YOUR TIME

A pony is a horse that is less than 4 feet, 10 inches tall from the top of its shoulders to its feet. Miniature horses are even smaller. In the United States, a horse can be no taller than 2 feet, 10 inches to qualify as miniature. Miniature horses often have features like full-size horses, whereas ponies may have a stockier appearance.

friendly animals

YOUR TIME

Gorillas can be found in central Africa. These gentle apes are close relatives of humans, chimpanzees, and bonobos. The critically endangered creatures are threatened by deforestation, poaching, and regional wars.

friendly animals

YOUR TIME

Cats were most likely first domesticated to keep rodents away from grain stores in the Middle East. Today there are nearly 90 million house cats in the United States—and many more standing guard in barns and stables.

friendly animals

Dogs and kids make perfect pals. Just look at these two.
But something's different in these pics—you know what to do!

YOUR TIME

This fluffy pup will grow into a high-energy working dog. Siberian huskies are descended from dogs bred by the Chukchi people, an indigenous group in northeastern Siberia, to pull sleds during harsh Arctic winters.

friendly animals

YOUR TIME

This tiny parrot is a budgie (short for *budgerigar*), a species of parakeet that originally came from Australia. While birds are excellent pets, they are not nearly as popular as dogs and cats. They are found in a little more than 3 percent of U.S. households. That may not sound like a lot, but it's more than 3.6 million homes!

friendly animals

Who did your hair? It's perfect. I need to get the name.
I just hope that when mine's done, we still look the same.

YOUR TIME

Javan langurs are native to the island of Java, in Indonesia. As many as 20 may live in a social group. These leaf-eating monkeys have slender bodies and long tails. In fact, *langur* means "long tail" in the Sanskrit language.

friendly animals

Lost among a sea of stripes on muzzles, flanks, and manes, find the things that really shouldn't be out on the plains.

YOUR TIME

Zebras find safety hiding among their friends. Their stripes make it harder for lions and hyenas to pick one animal out from the herd. But the stripes may help them in another way, too: Horseflies are not attracted to the kind of light reflected by a zebra's coat.

friendly animals

Stars and sun and ice-cream cone. My eyes are playing tricks!
Spot the changes, one by one, before he takes a lick.

YOUR TIME

Tempting though it may be to share your ice-cream cone with an adorable Dalmatian, it's best to keep it to yourself. Chocolate contains caffeine and theobromine, two substances that humans can handle, but that may make your pooch very sick.

friendly animals

YOUR TIME

This fluffy barred owl may look cuddly, but by night it is a deadly hunter. Like all owls, it has large wings for its body size. This allows the owl to stay in the air at slower speeds than other birds. Owls also have feathers with fluffy edges that break up the air. These features make for silent flight as the owls swoop in to capture prey.

friendly animals

Tigers might seem like your cat, but it is not true.
If you took them home one day, they'd surely gobble you!

YOUR TIME

Tigers are the largest cats in the world. They aren't really the friendliest of animals. Adults prefer to live and hunt alone, but young tigers will stay with their mothers until they are two or three years old and ready to strike out on their own.

friendly animals

YOUR TIME

Originally found in the Central and South American rain forest, highly social macaws can live in groups of up to 20 birds and form strong, lifelong bonds with their mates. Unfortunately, their popularity as pets has led to illegal trapping of wild birds. That, combined with habitat loss, has left some species of macaws critically endangered.

friendly animals

Can't find Mom? Maybe Fido wants to kitten-sit.
She'll rearrange the scenery, but we can live with it.

YOUR TIME

About 65 percent of U.S. households keep some kind of pet. About 44 percent of those households have dogs, and 35 percent have cats. But owners of cats are more likely to have more than one, so there are more cats than dogs in U.S. homes overall.

friendly animals

Let me whisper in your ear the rules of this change game:
We're different on the outside, but our insides stay the same.

YOUR TIME

Male ostriches can grow as tall as 9 feet and weigh up to 287 pounds, making them the largest birds on Earth. Giraffes are the tallest animals on Earth, with males growing up to 18 feet tall and weighing as much as 3,000 pounds.

friendly animals

YOUR TIME

African elephants can weigh 200 pounds at birth. By the time these baby buddies have grown, they could weigh as much as 14,000 pounds. So it's not surprising that adult elephants spend about 20 hours a day munching grass, leaves, and bark to keep their enormous bodies going.

friendly animals

Two monkey buddies sit among the trees.
There are changes high and low. Take a look—you'll see!

YOUR TIME 🕐

Rhesus macaques are often found close to humans in towns and villages throughout Asia. As a result, they get about 93 percent of their food from human sources. People feed them, and they also find food in trash cans and farmers' fields. They have large cheek pouches, a bit like a hamster's, that they can stuff full on scavenging trips.

friendly animals

What could be better than one wiggly pup? How about two?
Find all the changes in this scene—you'll have seven when you're through.

YOUR TIME

The number of puppies in a litter depends upon the breed. Labrador retrievers may have up to seven puppies at a time, while a normal litter of Pomeranians is one to three pups.

friendly animals

Hop onto his snout, and he'll give you a ride.
But be careful to make sure you stay on the outside!

YOUR TIME

Seven species of crocodiles live in warm, wet Indonesia, where this crocodile is providing taxi service for a toad. The toad is safe for now, but he wouldn't want to be on the other side of that snout. Crocodiles have some of the strongest bites in the world. A saltwater crocodile can snap its jaws closed with 4,000 pounds per square inch of force.

friendly animals

This handsome frog has changed his spots. So has the butterfly. But wait—we've changed up other things. How many can you spy?

YOUR TIME ⏱

Some frogs live in ponds, streams, and puddles. Others spend most of their lives in trees. Tree frogs, or arboreal frogs, can be found in forests throughout the world, but rain forests are often home to especially colorful and diverse species. This friendly frog lives in the rain forests of Indonesia.

friendly animals

In this pile of puppies, something doesn't match.
It's not just the baby—there are differences to catch!

YOUR TIME 🕐

Historians disagree on the origins of the French bulldog, but it is clear that these dogs are descended from English bulldogs. Most likely, the breed moved to France in the late 19th century when English workers moved there looking for work. Wherever they came from, they are irresistible as puppies and as grown dogs.

friendly animals

YOUR TIME

Cute and intelligent, bottlenose dolphins may be the friendliest mammals in the seas. They often travel in groups of up to 20 animals. The size of a group changes constantly as new dolphins join and others swim off on their own. Dolphins are fast swimmers, with a top speed of more than 20 miles per hour.

friendly animals

Little nighttime bandits peering from their hideout.
Can you sniff out the differences with your little snout?

YOUR TIME ⏲

A raccoon mother has two to five babies in her den. The family will stay cozy in the den through the winter, then the babies will strike out on their own the next spring.

friendly animals

Things aren't what they seem with these two macaws. What colors were they at the start—can you still recall?

YOUR TIME

These cuddly birds are green-winged macaws. Like other macaws, mating pairs of this species stay together for life. And their lives are very long—as long as 50 years in captivity. That's very friendly indeed.

friendly animals

He can see the right and left, and even in between, but do you think that he can spot what's changed in this scene?

YOUR TIME

Damselflies are brightly colored insects that are often mistaken for dragonflies. Like dragonflies, they begin life in the water, and as adults they are found near ponds and streams. How can you tell the difference? Dragonflies' wings stay apart when they are at rest, while damselflies' wings fold up over their backs.

funny animals

YOUR TIME

When a dog rolls onto its back, it could be saying many things. It might be backing down to a superior rival, or getting into a better position to defend itself from attack. Then again, it might just be asking for a belly rub.

funny animals

Changes, changes, everywhere—gear up for winter weather.
Grab a beanie and your scarf, and put on your warmest sweater!

YOUR TIME

The guinea pig's ancestors were cavies, wild rodents native to South America. Spanish explorers brought guinea pigs to Europe in the 16th century, and they became popular pets.

funny animals

Smiling for the camera, this goat is saying, "Cheese!"
You can spot the differences, but only if you please.

YOUR TIME

Male goats, known as bucks or billies, typically have beards. Female goats, known as does, give birth to babies, called kids. The process of giving birth is called kidding. No joke!

funny animals

Let's go riding in the car—we'll enjoy the breeze.
Then you can spot the changes, as easy as you please!

YOUR TIME

Basset hounds are hunting dogs. They are perfectly suited for following scents. Their short legs keep them close to the ground. Their long ears stir up animals' trails, wafting the smell toward their noses.

funny animals

YOUR TIME

Sand tiger sharks, despite their ragged teeth and menacing appearance, are actually quite docile. They rarely attack humans unless they feel threatened. Sand tigers are the only species of shark known to swim to the surface for air. Holding the air in their stomachs allows them to stay still while they wait for prey.

funny animals

YOUR TIME 🕐

Many animals have backbones, and many have shells, but a turtle is the only animal that has both a backbone and a shell. Turtle shells are made up of bones that are covered by plates. The plates, called scutes, are made of keratin, the same substance in human fingernails.

funny animals

Grab your raincoat and your boots. It's time to take a walk.
But first let's find the changes here. If only dogs could talk.

YOUR TIME

There is a wider range of sizes and shapes in domestic dogs than in any other species of animal. The largest Great Dane in the world, named Freddy, is 3 feet, 4 inches tall from the top of his shoulder to the ground. Chihuahuas, the smallest dogs, are generally 9 inches tall.

funny animals

Is there something in my teeth? Should I floss a little more?
How many differences can you find? Are you keeping score?

YOUR TIME

Male zebras, like male horses, are called stallions. Females are called mares, and their babies are called foals. Constant grass grazing wears zebras' teeth down. Luckily for them, their teeth never stop growing.

funny animals

YOUR TIME

Elephants' large ears serve as giant coolers. As elephants flap their ears, the blood in veins below the skin's surface is cooled by moving air. The action reduces body temperature by several degrees. How cool is that?

funny animals

This pair of party animals is here to test your eyes.
If you can find eight differences, they will yell, "SURPRISE!"

YOUR TIME

On average, cats live about 3 years longer than dogs. The average dog life span is 12 years, while the average cat life span is 15 years. The record for oldest cat is held by Crème Puff, who lived to 38 years old. The oldest dog, Bluey, lived to be 29.

funny animals

This tree frog's sticking out his tongue—some may say that's rude.
Can you spot all the differences before he eats his food?

YOUR TIME

Red-eyed tree frogs, native to the Central American rain forest, are best known for their big, bright red eyes, which they use to frighten predators. Their suction-cup toes help them climb trees and attach to leaves, where they wait for food. Their meals of choice? Insects, including crickets, moths, flies, and grasshoppers, of course!

funny animals

YOUR TIME 🕐

Many people think of cats as aloof. Yet half the cats in a behavior study preferred spending time with humans over eating or playing. Maybe dogs aren't man's only best friends.

funny animals

I'm changing up my coat with some colorful spots.
That's not all that's different, though—bet YOU can find lots!

YOUR TIME

Built for swimming, Labrador retrievers have webbed toes to help them paddle. Used by U.S. hunters as field dogs since the early 19th century, they also became beloved family dogs. In fact, they have been number one in the American Kennel Club's ranking of most popular dogs for more than 20 years.

funny animals

Ladybugs, or lady beetles, are best known for their spots.
But that's not all that's different here—look beyond their dots.

YOUR TIME

Ladybugs are also known as ladybird beetles or lady beetles. Surprisingly, not all ladybugs have spots. Some species are striped, while others have no markings at all. In many cultures, ladybugs are a sign of good luck.

funny animals

When it's hot outside, what else can a monkey do?
He'll sit and have a popsicle while you find out what's new.

YOUR TIME

Monkeys can be divided into two major groups. Old World monkeys, such as this rhesus macaque, are found in Africa and Asia. They have longer noses, with nostrils that face down or forward. New World monkeys are found in Central and South America and Mexico. They have short noses, and tails that can be used for grasping and climbing.

funny animals

YOUR TIME

Long before Boo the Pomeranian took over the Internet, a Scottish terrier named Fala became the first celebrity dog. Fala belonged to President Franklin Roosevelt. Since then, there have been many famous First Dogs—including Millie, who belonged to George H.W. Bush, and Bo and Sunny, who belong to Barack Obama.

funny animals

You might find this surprising, but pigs can be quite clean.
Can you spot all the differences in this cute little scene?

YOUR TIME

Contrary to popular belief, pigs are not dirty animals. Why the bad rap? They can't sweat, so they roll in the mud to cool off. And their muddy habit has many other benefits. It protects their skin from sunburn, insect bites, and harmful parasites.

funny animals

A giraffe on a tightrope—what a sight to see!
Count up all the changes while she defies gravity.

YOUR TIME

With their long legs and lengthy necks, giraffes are the world's tallest land animals. A giraffe's neck measures 6 feet and weighs up to 600 pounds. Its heart measures 2 feet and can weigh up to 25 pounds. That is a big heart!

funny animals

This dog is chilling at the beach, where it's sandy and it's hot. Can you find all the differences? How many can you spot?

YOUR TIME

Dogs can't sweat like humans do to keep cool. When it's hot outside, they pant to lower their body temperature. Some breeds, like pugs and bulldogs, pant more frequently because of their short snouts.

funny animals

It's playtime for this dolphin; he'd like a game of catch.
Look at these two pictures, and find what doesn't match.

YOUR TIME

At aquariums around the country, bottlenose dolphins are great entertainers because they are smart, friendly, charismatic, and easy to train. Because the corners of their mouths are slightly upturned, dolphins appear to be always smiling. Bottlenose dolphins can jump, or breach, up to 16 feet out of water. That makes quite a splash!

funny animals

YOUR TIME

Hares and rabbits, even though they belong to the same family, are actually quite different. Hares are less social than rabbits, for one. Rabbits are born without fur and with their eyes closed, while hares are born with fur and with their eyes open. Both rabbits and hares have several large litters of babies every year.

funny animals

This Frenchie is cruising, driving her new car.
Find all the changes before she drives too far!

YOUR TIME

The French bulldog (*Frenchie* for short) was officially recognized by the American Kennel Club in 1898. It is the sixth most popular dog breed today. Lady Gaga, Hugh Jackman, John Legend and Chrissy Teigen, and Reese Witherspoon are just a few celebrities who have owned French bulldogs.

funny animals

This monkey is quite hungry—he's hoarding all his fruit. Help him look for all the changes, even the most minute.

YOUR TIME

Monkeys can use their hands and feet for gripping branches or food. Their feet are just as flexible as their hands, which they use for climbing throughout the rain forest. Some monkeys can even swim, using their partially webbed feet to help them move in the water.

funny animals

YOUR TIME

Raccoons are extremely dexterous animals. They use their long front paws to find food. The clever creatures have been known to open trash cans, windows, and even locks. But this may be the first raccoon to put on his own tie!

funny animals

This fuzzy orange guy is playing peekaboo with you.
But something tells me that he's hiding other things, too!

YOUR TIME

Orangutans are tree-dwelling apes found only in Borneo and Sumatra. They can be as tall as 5 feet and weigh as much as 180 pounds. Despite their size, they move gracefully through the treetops with the help of long arms measuring 7 feet from fingertip to fingertip. Each night, they make new beds out of bent branches and leaves to stay safe and snug.

funny animals

There's a new sheriff in town, and he's on the prowl.
Find all the changes, or he's going to growl!

YOUR TIME

It's not unusual for dogs and cats to have serious jobs. Dogs serve in search-and-rescue operations, on police and military teams, and on bomb squads. They work with livestock on farms, as aids in hunting, and as assistance and therapy animals. For thousands of years, cats have been keeping disease-carrying rodents out of barns and houses.

solutions

Ready to check your work? Find the page number below that corresponds to your puzzle. We've circled the changes for you. Were you stumped? Don't worry—you can try again with the next one!

4

6

8

10

12

14

16

18

20

22

24

26

28

30

32

34

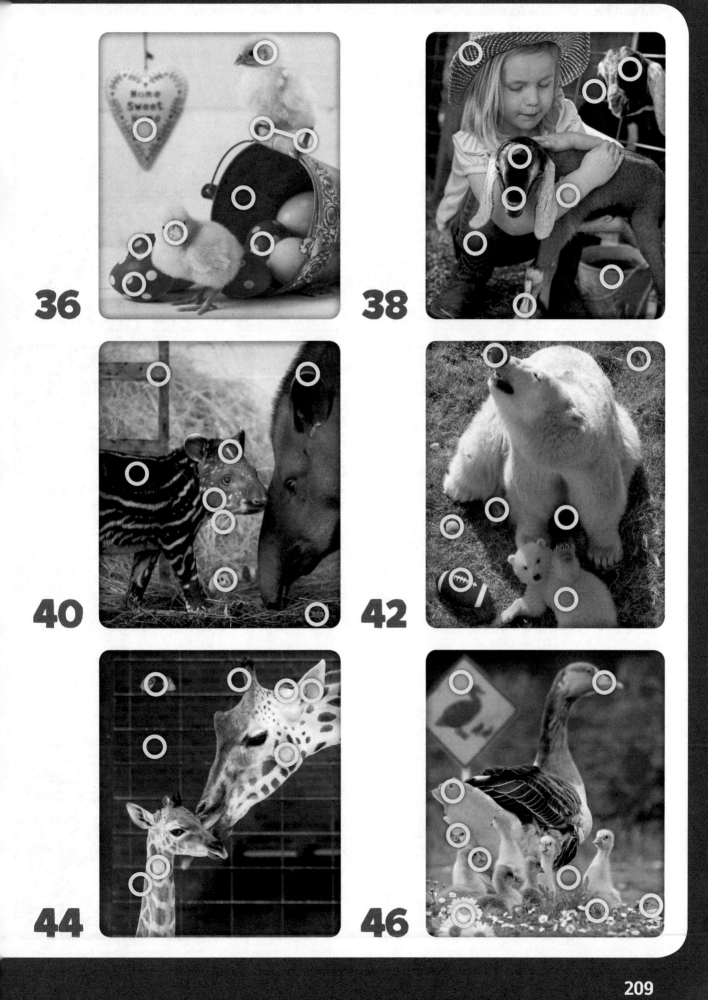

36

38

40

42

44

46

48

50

52

54

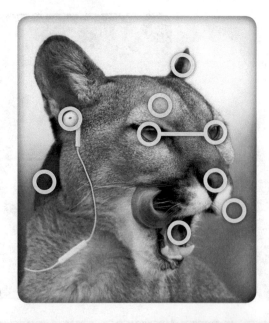

56

58

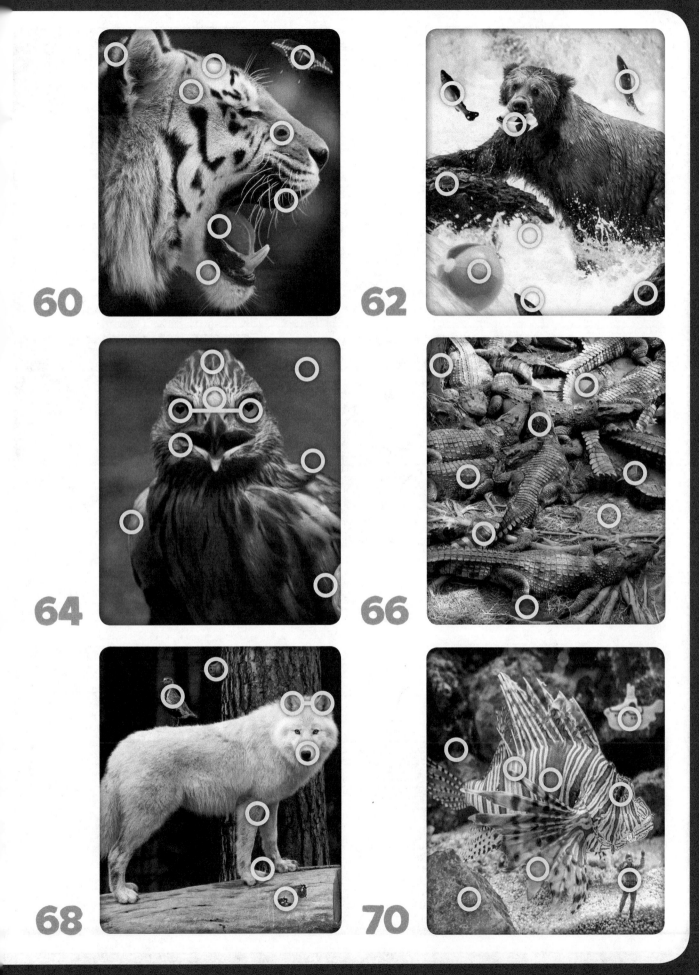

60

62

64

66

68

70

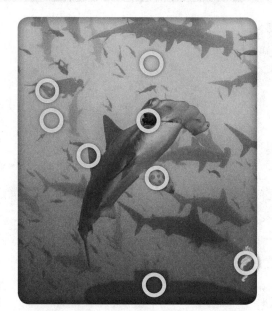

72

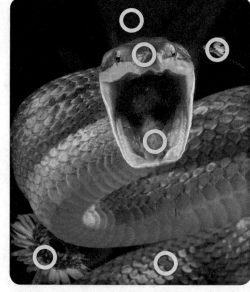

74

76

78

80

82

204

picture credits

All images Shutterstock.com, with the exception of the following:

Pages 1: Retales Botijero/Getty Images; 3: Retales Botijero/Getty Images; 4–5: Brandon Kidwell/Getty Images; 11: (scarf) Charlie Abad/Getty Images, (hat) Retales Botijero/Getty Images, (sunglasses) Chet W/Getty Images; 13: (dandelion) Diana Miller/Getty Images; 15: (hat) Fernando Trabanco Fotografia/ Getty Images; 17: (magnolia blossoms) Bruno Crescia Photography Inc./Getty Images; 29: (scarf) Topic Images Inc./Getty Images, (flowers) I love Photo and Apple/GettyImages; 36–37: FikMik/Getty Images; 38–39: TerryJ/Getty Images; 40–41: AFP/Getty Images; 42–43: Valery Hache/Getty Images, (football) TRITOOTH/Getty Images; 44–45: ullstein bild/Getty Images; 46–47: Arterra/Getty Images; 48–49: Chris Ison/PA Images/Getty Images; 55: (boxing gloves) payathep/Getty images; 63: (flat soccer ball) Fuse/Getty Images; 84–85: Tom Bean/Getty Images; 86–87: Millard H Sharp/Getty Images; 104–105: Darrell Gulin/Getty Images; 105: (caterpillar) arlindo71/Getty Images; 107: (collar) mehmettorlak/ Getty Images, (monarch butterfly) Liliboas/Getty Images, (painted lady butterfly and yellow flower) Sabine Thielemann/EyeEm/Getty Images; 115: (bandanna) ~UserGI15633745/Getty Images; 122–123: SolStock/Getty Images; 140–141: shikheigoh/Getty Images; 142–143: kuritafsheen/Getty Images; 144–145: Andrew Bret Wallis/Getty Images; 155: (balloon) Dorling Kindersley/Getty Images; 157: (sunglasses) Chet W/Getty Images, (running shoes) flyfloor/Getty Images; 163: (watery background) Ippei Naoi/Getty Images, (swim cap) Uwe Krejci/Getty Images; 191: (coconut drink) mphillips007/Getty Images; 205: (sheriff hat) Tom Chance/Getty Images, (pearl necklace) Tarzhanova/Getty Images.

These party animals want to thank you for joining our puzzle party! Check out these other fun books, available now.

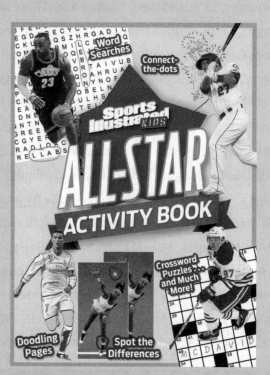

Big Book of WHY Activity Book
978-1-68330-757-0 $9.99 US/$11.99 CAN

All-Star Activity Book
978-1-68330-773-0 $9.99 US/$11.99 CAN